FIRST REPERTOIRE F
VIOLIN
violin part

CONTENTS

FABER ff **MUSIC**

Gavottes I and II

from *Suite in D BWV 1068*

Johann Sebastian Bach

Gavotte I

Gavotte II

Bourrée

from *Flute Sonata No.3*

George Frideric Handel

Searching for Lambs

Traditional arr. Cecil Sharp

Andantino

from *Six Easy Pieces Op.22*

Edward Elgar

Lean, Mean Tango

Mary Cohen

Menuets I and II

from *Music for the Royal Fireworks*

George Frideric Handel

© 2006 by Faber Music Ltd.

Allegro

from *Serenade No. 1*

Wolfgang Amadeus Mozart

© 2006 by Faber Music Ltd.

Polka

from *Little School of Melody Op.123*

Charles Dancla

Impromptu

Cornelius Gurlitt

Puttin' on the Ritz

Irving Berlin

Glitzy and determined! ♩ = 80

Introduction and Rondo

from *Little School of Melody Op.123*

Charles Dancla

Introduction

Andante maestoso ♩ = c.72

Rondo

Night Flight

Mary Cohen

Andante

from *Sonatina No.4 Op.48*

Ignace Pleyel

Barn Dance

Cornelius Gurlitt

The Pink Panther

Henry Mancini

FIRST REPERTOIRE FOR
VIOLIN

with piano

edited, selected and arranged by

Mary Cohen

© 2006 by Faber Music Ltd
This edition first published in 2006 by Faber Music Ltd
3 Queen Square, London WC1N 3AU
Music processed by Jackie Leigh
Cover illustration by Drew Hillier
Cover design by Matthew Lee
Printed in England by Caligraving Ltd
All rights reserved
ISBN 0-571-52497-4

To buy Faber Music publications or to find out about the full range of titles available
please contact your local music retailer or Faber Music sales enquiries:

Faber Music Limited, Burnt Mill, Elizabeth Way, Harlow, CM20 2HX England
Tel: +44 (0)1279 82 89 82   Fax: +44 (0)1279 82 89 83
sales@fabermusic.com   fabermusic.com

CONTENTS

Gavottes I and II
from *Suite in D BWV 1068*

Johann Sebastian Bach

Gavotte I

4

Gavotte II

Gavotte I da Capo

Bourrée

from *Flute Sonata No.3*

George Frideric Handel

Searching for Lambs

Traditional arr. Cecil Sharp

Andantino
from *Six Easy Pieces Op.22*

Edward Elgar

Lean, Mean Tango

Mary Cohen

Menuets I and II

from *Music for the Royal Fireworks*

George Frideric Handel

Menuet I

Moderato ♩ = *c.*116

Menuet II

Menuet I da Capo

Allegro

from *Serenade No.1*

Wolfgang Amadeus Mozart

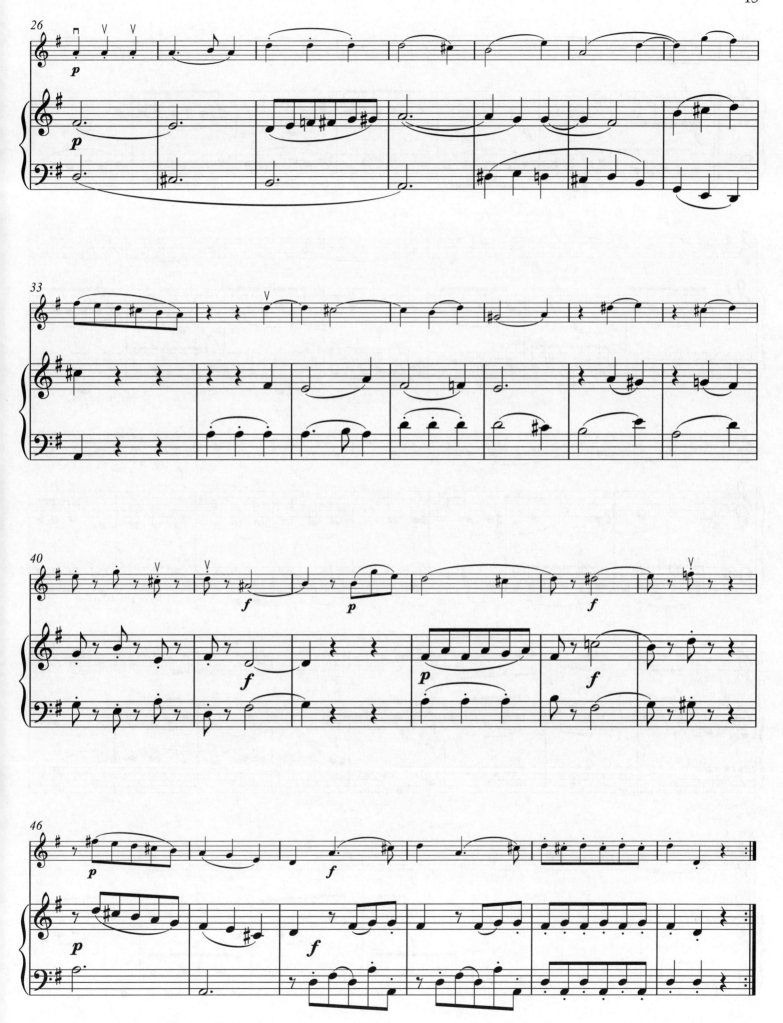

Polka
from *Little School of Melody Op.123*

Charles Dancla

Impromptu

Cornelius Gurlitt

Puttin' on the Ritz

Irving Berlin

Introduction and Rondo

from *Little School of Melody Op.123*

Charles Dancla

Introduction

Night Flight

Mary Cohen

Andante

from *Sonatina No.4 Op.48*

Ignace Pleyel

Barn Dance

Cornelius Gurlitt

The Pink Panther

Henry Mancini

VIOLIN MUSIC FROM FABER MUSIC

Up-Grade!
Light relief between grades
PAM WEDGWOOD

GRADES 1–2 ISBN 0-571-51954-7
GRADES 2–3 ISBN 0-571-51955-5

Violin All Sorts
*Great assortments of pieces
to pick and mix*
selected and edited by MARY COHEN

INITIAL–GRADE 1 ISBN 0-571-52227-0
GRADES 2–3 ISBN 0-571-52228-9

Fingerprints
*Easy contemporary pieces for the
Grade 1–4 standard player*
edited by MARY COHEN

ISBN 0-571-52258-0

Got those Position Blues?
*Nine jazzy pieces for violin and piano
in 2nd, 3rd and 4th positions*
EDWARD HUWS JONES

ISBN 0-571-51534-7

Gypsy Jazz
*Songs and dances from across
Europe for violin and piano*
POLLY WATERFIELD
and TIMOTHY KRAEMER

EASY LEVEL ISBN 0-571-51637-8
INTERMEDIATE LEVEL ISBN 0-571-51937-7

Jazzin' About
*Fun pieces for
violin and piano*
PAM WEDGWOOD

ISBN 0-571-51315-8